Original title:
Life: So Many Questions, So Few Answers

Copyright © 2025 Creative Arts Management OÜ
All rights reserved.

Author: Wyatt Kensington
ISBN HARDBACK: 978-1-80566-222-8
ISBN PAPERBACK: 978-1-80566-517-5

Chasing After Shadows

I sprint through halls where shadows play,
But every turn, they slip away.
I ask the cat, who seems to know,
He stretches wide, then steals the show.

Why do socks always disappear?
I'm pretty sure they're living here.
In secret lands of fur and fluff,
Where maybes reign, and truths are tough.

The Silent Pursuit of Truth

I knock on doors of wisdom's dome,
But often find they're just for show.
The wise old owl just blinks and stares,
While squirrels plot with fanciful airs.

Truth feels like a game of charades,
Where all the players silently fade.
I roll my eyes, they chirp and coo,
Hey, someone get me a clearer view!

Puzzle Pieces of Existence

I gathered pieces, bright and bold,
But none fit well, or so I'm told.
The corner ones are chewed and torn,
By curious pets at early dawn.

I once found one that looked like cheese,
Thought, perhaps, it's just meant to tease.
The picture's blurry, colors blend,
I'm not sure I'll reach the end!

Dances with Doubt

I tango with the doubts that creep,
They whisper problems in my sleep.
I grab a partner, spin around,
But tripping feels like solid ground.

Each question hops and skips away,
As if to say, 'Not today, okay?'
I laugh aloud, it's quite a show,
In my dance hall of "I don't know!"

In the Labyrinth of Thought

Why do we park on driveways, just to walk on the street?
And if a fly falls in soup, is it still a treat?
When did a round pizza come in a square box?
And why is it that we call it 'hamster' when it's just a tiny fox?

Questions spin like a dizzy top, oh what a show,
Why do they put locks on public restrooms, we don't know?
If two's company and three's a crowd, who's on the list?
Sometimes, I think even the answers have missed!

Unraveled Threads

Why does the sun never get tired of rising?
And what's the deal with birds, always advertising?
Who decides the price of things in the grocery aisle?
And how can a cat be so aloof, yet still beguile?

When do socks vanish, where do they escape?
And why does toast land butter-side down, in this shape?
If we're not supposed to eat midnight snacks with glee,
Then why is the fridge so inviting to me?

Beneath the Surface

Do fish get thirsty, sipping waves on the go?
What are clouds made of, can anyone know?
If humans can't breathe underwater, why swim like a fish?
And what's the deal with all these flavors of jelly, I wish!

Does a hippo sweat when it gets too hot?
Where do the lost socks and spoons go when we trot?
If ghosts can haunt, do they get hungry too?
What a peculiar world, with questions anew!

Silent Queries

If we're all made of stardust, why don't we shine?
And is it really true that spaghetti can climb?
When did we start measuring time with a clock?
And if knowledge is power, is ignorance a rock?

What do you call a funny situation, my dear?
If a joke's not funny, is it just a sneer?
And when you find answers, do more questions arise?
Oh, the riddles of life are quite the surprise!

A Tapestry of Thoughts

In a world filled with chatter,
I pondered a squirrel's flight.
Does it know where it's going?
Or just winging it—what a sight!

A shoelace untied, I trip and fall,
Maybe the ground has secrets to tell.
Why is cheese so good with it all?
I guess some questions won't ring a bell.

The Silent Symphony

An orchestra plays, but I hear no sound,
The dog looks puzzled, with head at an angle.
Is he sensing the music I'm not around?
Or lost in the thought of a bone just dangled?

My coffee's gone cold, yet thoughts bubble hot,
Why is the sky blue while I'm stuck in gray?
If toast lands butter-side down, is it fate or a plot?
Perhaps it's just breakfast that's gone astray.

An Odyssey of Whys

Why do socks go missing in the wash?
Is there a secret world where they all play?
Conversations with plants seem sublime—
Do they gossip about us at the end of the day?

Cars beep and humans shout, what's the big fuss?
Are we all just players in a well-scripted play?
With stars overhead, I ponder and fuss,
Wonder if they chuckle at our clumsy ballet.

Reflections in the Fog

Peering through mist, I ask who's to blame,
For the lost umbrella of quirky design?
Did it flee to a place with a better name?
With answers elusive, I sip my cold brine.

Clouds roll in with inquiries of their own,
Why can't I dance like a leaf on the breeze?
As questions mount high like a trophy stone,
I just laugh, plop down, and munch on some peas.

Wings of Inquiry

Why do birds always sing?
When cats just sit and stare.
Questions float on gentle wings,
While answers vanish in thin air.

Do socks really disappear?
Or do they just make a break?
Where's the button on my gear?
Did the coffee pot just quake?

Why do we laugh at bad puns?
Is it joy or sheer disdain?
Life's a joke that never runs,
Yet we're stuck with half the grain.

So let's dance with silly doubts,
Twirl around while we confide.
In the midst of twirling bouts,
We find humor as our guide.

Mirrors of Reflection

Why do mirrors always lie?
Am I really that round?
When I smile, do they comply?
Or do they just make a sound?

How many faces can I show?
Is there one that's really me?
With each glance, I see them glow,
Yet I'm still lost at sea.

Am I older than I seem?
Or just a trick of the shade?
In my dreams, I knit a theme,
But awake, I'm just delayed.

When I ponder, time stands still,
While my snacks are calling loud.
Do I chase dreams or a thrill?
Or just munch with a proud crowd?

The Sound of Silence

Is silence just a clever ploy?
To trick us into the hush?
When I ponder, do birds enjoy?
Or is chatter their daily crush?

It speaks a language rich and clear,
Though we often miss the signs.
Why do whispers bring such cheer?
Are they secrets or designs?

In stillness, questions dart and play,
Like squirrels skittering around.
Is there music in the gray?
Or just crickets with no sound?

In the quiet, laughter sneaks,
As answers barely take a seat.
Life's a riddle; oh, it tweaks,
With humor that can't be beat.

Vastness of What We Don't Know

Why is the universe so vast?
Are there neighbors we could meet?
Or is it just a cosmic cast,
With black holes as our retreat?

Do aliens ponder like we do?
Or do they laugh at our plight?
In a world where odd is true,
Their spaceships might take flight.

How do fish perceive the sky?
Are they plotting their escape?
Is it just a wish or lie?
Swimming laps in their own tape?

In the depths of unknown lore,
We find giggles, truths untold.
While we ponder the great score,
We discover we're quite bold.

The Search for Solidity

In a world where socks go missing,
And keys play hide and seek,
I ponder grand dilemmas,
Like why my plants are weak.

Why does my cat look guilty,
When I find a mess he made?
Do they think we're on a sitcom,
Or just stars in a parade?

I question love and purpose,
What's the point of cereal?
Are we lost in some big puzzle,
Or just stuck in a reel?

So I'll toast to all the queries,
And sip my tea with glee,
For every laugh and quandary,
Is just a part of me.

Waves of Wonder

Why does toast always land butter side down?
Is it a conspiracy to take the crown?
Do socks really vanish in the wash?
Or do they party with keys, feeling posh?

Why does the cat knock over my drink?
Is it their way of making me think?
When did the sun decide to blaze?
And why does it choose to set in a haze?

If chairs could talk, what would they say?
Would they gossip 'bout us every day?
Do fish get bored of swimming in schools?
Or do they make the same classic jokes as fools?

Maybe the world is just one big riddle,
And we're all stuck in a cosmic middle.
But with a laugh and a quirky dance,
We'll face the questions and take a chance.

Whispered Mysteries

Why do we chase the ice cream truck's song?
Yet the napkin's the one that takes way too long?
Is cereal a soup? Can we please decide?
And why do we run from shoes we can't abide?

Do ants have meetings? What do they discuss?
Is it slip and slide or simply a fuss?
Why does sleep seem to steal the best hours?
And who said we can't talk to flowers?

If clouds had faces, would they frown or beam?
Or whisper secrets in a dreamer's dream?
Do books sometimes wish to roam on their own?
Or are pages content to just sit and moan?

With giggles and grins, we ponder away,
In this thrilling game we play each day.
Perhaps the mysteries, both big and small,
Are meant to amuse and make us all—fall.

The Echo of Uncertainty

Is it just me, or do plants like to stare?
As if they're judging my lack of flair.
Why do we talk to ourselves in the mirror?
Is it because our own voices are clearer?

Do dogs hold debates with their tails each night?
Arguing over who's wrong or right?
When a phone rings, why do we jump and squeak?
Is that alert hidden in the peek?

If mirrors could gossip, what tales would they weave?
About the secrets we hide up our sleeves?
Do clouds ever argue about shapes they make?
Or do they just float, for goodness' sake?

With every question, we giggle and fret,
A bubbling cauldron of curious debt.
Embrace the echoes, the funny and strange,
For answers, my friends, are bound to change!

Chasing Fleeting Shadows

Why does the fridge light only glow when we peek?
Is it shy in the day, just too proud to sneak?
Why do we look for things in the wrong place?
Like searching for socks in a cereal space?

Why do we laugh at our own silly slips?
Yet never think twice about cat meme trips?
If clouds could dance, would they waltz or spin?
Or would they just drift while wearing a grin?

Do time machines work on coffee and cake?
Or is that a myth a sleepy mind makes?
When a shadow runs, where does it go?
Like ancient secrets we'll never know!

So here's to the fun of the questions we chase,
Each silly thought with a smile on its face.
In chasing shadows, we find delight,
And the humor in fragments, both day and night.

The Tapestry of Doubt

Woven threads of what-ifs, so bright,
Unraveling truths, out of sight.
Each stitch pulls tight, then lets it go,
And I wonder if I'll ever know.

Looms of yarn in a tangled mess,
I ask for answers, they just guess.
What color is confusion? Odds are high,
It's a mix of laughter and a sigh.

With each knot, a story unfolds,
But who needs clarity? It's getting old!
I'll wear my doubts like a fancy hat,
Yet scrunches fine when I sit down flat.

So here I am, in fabric tight,
Questioning all beneath the light.
But if answers wore polka dots,
I'd probably trade them for some pots!

Dreams of the Unknown

Last night I dreamed of flying high,
On a giant taco in the sky.
But when I asked it for a clue,
It just said, 'Eh, you're on your own, dude.'

Chasing shadows in a colorful race,
Each curve and twist gives me a face.
I stop to ask, 'What's the big deal?'
The shadows chuckle, I barely feel.

Wrestling thoughts like wriggly worms,
Every question bends, squiggles, squirms.
Can I toggle the truth like a light?
Or is that just part of my flight?

With each passing thought, I take a spin,
In this nonsense game, will I ever win?
Maybe the prize is more of this whim,
Riding the waves of dreams, on a whim.

Frayed Edges of Curiosity

My mind is a quilt with edges worn,
Patching ideas I've over-sown.
Each question's a patch, a quirky design,
Frayed edges, but who needs to align?

Curiosity's a cat, or so they say,
But mine is more of a puppy's play.
Chasing tails of thoughts that never settle,
With a yappy bark, I press the pedal.

Knots of wonder twist and twirl,
Each loop a mystery, each curl a whirl.
Scratching my head, I ponder away,
While the universe chuckles, 'Just play!'

So let's roll in this joyous mess,
Questions are gems, I must confess.
With frayed edges dancing in the breeze,
Every uncertainty's a chance to tease.

The Space Between Answers

In the gap where wisdom might reside,
Lies a marshmallow of thoughts, too wide.
I reach for answers but it's quite a tease,
They hide behind giggles and a sneeze.

Like two socks lost in the laundry's spin,
I search for meaning, what a win!
The rubber duck floats with a knowing grin,
And whispers, 'Just laugh, let the fun begin!'

Questions linger like a song so sweet,
Sipping tea at a roundabout seat.
Oh, what's the rush? In time I will see,
That the space between is part of the spree.

So here I sit, in the awkward pause,
In the dance of not knowing, I find my cause.
Each chuckle and snort is a step in the dance,
Embracing the unknown as part of the chance.

The Quest for Clarity

Why's the sky so big and blue?
Is it made of paint or just a view?
Do dogs think we're just as clever?
Or do they plot to take us ever?

Why do socks vanish in the wash?
Do they join a club? Whoosh, whoosh, whoosh!
Is coffee made by wizards' hands?
Or just a bean from distant lands?

If time flies, does it wear a cape?
And if I drop it, can it escape?
Do breezes gossip with the trees?
Or do they just enjoy a tease?

What's the secret to the perfect pie?
Do secrets simmer? Oh my, oh my!
Will we find out before we age?
Or is it stuck on some lost page?

Threads of Inquiry

Why does butter always slide?
Is it scared of being fried?
Do cats really think they rule?
Or are they simply playing cool?

Why do we talk to inanimate things?
Are they listening? Do they have wings?
Do ants hold meetings out of sight?
Plotting world domination at night?

If I ask my goldfish about the stars,
Will he ponder deep or just swim far?
Do shadows chat when no one's near?
Witty banter or just sheer fear?

Why does cereal always go soft?
Does it cry when it gets tossed?
Is the fridge a cold, dark bar?
Serving dreams and leftovers afar?

Starlit Questions

Do stars giggle up in the sky?
Or are they just too shy to tie?
If the moon had a favorite song,
Would it sing it all night long?

Why do we fear the things unknown?
Are they simply brightly grown?
If a tree falls, does it yawn too?
Or is it a dance with the great dew?

Can marshmallows really ride a comet?
Or are they stuck in a sweet, warm closet?
Do clouds fluff-puff in a fairytale?
Or simply float as boats set sail?

What's a snail think while it crawls?
Is it dreaming of grand cat calls?
Do crickets hold a nightly ball?
With serenades, they can enthrall!

The Dance of Doubt

Why do we trip on unseen shoelaces?
Are they plotting mischievous paces?
Do mirrors giggle when we make faces?
Or do they just enjoy our traces?

If hiccups are whispers from the soul,
Why do they come in a row and stroll?
What does the fridge hum in the night?
A melody lost in the fridge's fright?

If fish could dance, how would it go?
A waltz or a tango? We do not know!
Do bubbles have a secret life?
Floating dreams without any strife?

Why is the remote always out of reach?
Is it learning from lessons that we teach?
Do clouds ever wish to change their hue?
Or simply bask in the endless blue?

Shadows of Curiosity

Why does toast always land down?
Is it buttered or is it brown?
The cat looks wise, but it just purrs,
While I ponder my missing socks and spurs.

Why do we park in drive-thrus?
And I still can't find my old shoes?
The goldfish stares, deep in his bowl,
Judging my choices, oh what a role!

Why does the fridge hum at night?
When I check, it's just our friend's light.
The clock ticks loud, but moves so slow,
Am I late for a bus? I don't even know!

So many wonders, tangled in glee,
The world's a riddle, come laugh with me!

Between the Lines of Inquiry

If a tree falls, does it make a sound?
Or is the squirrel laughing all around?
Why is my dog the best at hide and seek?
He's always there, yet never speaks.

At the store, what's the deal with queues?
Are we waiting for answers or just new shoes?
Why do we call it a TV remote?
It never comes close to what I wrote.

Can I bake a cake with just one egg?
Or will it turn into a dancing peg?
The kitchen sings with pots and pans,
But dinner results never go as planned.

Questions linger like a buzzing bee,
Maybe the answers are just too funny!

Faded Footprints

Why do my footprints wash away?
Will they return after the play?
I chased my dreams down to the shore,
But they ran faster, what's in store?

Why do ducks always waddle by?
Is there a secret in their pie?
I tried to quack, but ended in squeaks,
Now I can't join their social peaks.

Why do people talk to their pets?
What deep confessions do they get?
With a cocked head and a playful bark,
My dog knows more than just a park.

Every trace leads me to a smile,
In this silly world, let's jest a while!

The Spectrum of Unknowing

What's the reason for a silly hat?
Do we wear them to feel less fat?
The fish in a bowl gives a watery stare,
While I question why no one cares.

Why do we say, 'kick the bucket'?
Is there a time when we must tuck it?
The mouse in the cupboard looks so cheesy,
Where's my snack, this feels quite uneasy!

How come socks disappear in the wash?
Is it a magic trick, or is it posh?
Laundry tales are filled with lore,
But I lost my sense of what's in store!

So let's ponder with laughter and jest,
In the chaos of questions, we find our zest!

Searching for Answers in Silence

In the quiet, I sit and ponder,
Questions rise and voices wander.
Why did the chicken cross the street?
To find the answer, oh what a feat!

I asked the tree, it just stood still,
No wisdom there, a complete nil.
The cat just laughed, a little too loud,
As I searched for truths in a fluffy cloud.

The stars twinkled, a distant tease,
Why do we trip over fallen leaves?
The moon just winked, as if to say,
Some tricks are fun and should stay that way.

Faces of Dilemmas

Socks unmatched, a classic plight,
Which one to wear, the left or right?
My coffee's cold, should I microwave?
But what if it turns into a wave?

I ponder pizza, with toppings galore,
But what if mushrooms just start to snore?
Should I dance like no one's there?
Or just sit still, pretending to care?

A lizard darts, where did it go?
Now I'm the one who's moving slow.
Should I chase it, or let it be?
It's probably happier, I'd agree!

The Opaque Mirror

I looked in a mirror, what did I see?
A face full of questions starring back at me.
Who wrote the manual on aging grace?
If I find it, will I join a race?

Is that a wrinkle, or just a smile?
That mirror's humor is truly worthwhile.
Oh, why do we judge by the outside skin?
Can't we just look for the laughter within?

An old photo pops, it gives me a fright,
With fashion choices that cause pure delight.
Is my past a jest, or just a tease?
I'll ask the mirror, but it's sure to freeze!

Strands of Uncertainty

I tried to braid my thoughts this morn,
But curls of doubt just seem to scorn.
Is that a strand of silver or gray?
Oh, should I just color it all away?

What socks do I wear, should they match my tie?
Or mix it up, like sprinkles in pie?
A puzzle of choices, a jumbled mess,
In the search for order, I must confess.

I'll buy a plant, it's good for the mood,
But what if it's shy and just wants food?
Should I name it Fred or call it Sue?
Each choice creates worry, oh what to do?

The Storm of Questions

Why does toast always land face down?
Is it a joke or a cosmic frown?
Do socks conspire to disappear?
Maybe it's all part of a larger sphere.

Are cats secretly plotting their reign?
Why does coffee never taste the same?
Can you measure the weight of a thought?
Or is it just something that can't be caught?

If I use a pencil, is it a sketch?
Or just a scribble, a mental fetch?
What defines what's wrong or what's right?
Could it be just a matter of sight?

When the fridge hums, does it tell tales?
Or is it just air in the food trails?
Should we trust all the signs on the way?
Or laugh till they dance and join the play?

Captivated by Inquiry

If I talk to my shoes, will they reply?
Or just sit there, silent, and shy?
What if goldfish hold parties at night?
Are they gossiping or swimming in fright?

Why do we yawn when we see others do?
Is it a virus, a friendly cue?
What's the meaning of a blinking light?
A signal of danger, or just a delight?

Do jellybeans know they're a treat?
Or wish they had legs and could dance on their feet?
If clouds complain about their weight,
Is it too heavy or just first-rate?

What's the deal with the universe's tune?
Is it humming to secrets of the moon?
Could a banana find love in a tree?
That would be quite a sight, don't you see?

The Echo Chamber of Thought

In the rooms of my mind, echoes stay,
Bouncing around in a quirky ballet.
Do fish hold conferences in the sea?
Or is that just how they let it be?

What do crickets discuss in their song?
The latest gossip or where they belong?
If clocks could talk, would they tick-tock slow?
Or would they race as they watch us go?

When I ponder life's mysteries right,
Do stars giggle at such a sight?
Is a puddle a portal to worlds unseen?
Or merely a splash where we've all been?

Could a potato be king of the spuds?
Ruling from fields of mud and floods?
What if questions were treasure to seek?
Would the answers tease or just make us weak?

Maps with No Destination

I drew a map with circles and lines,
But got lost in a tangle of signs.
Each 'X' I marked led me astray,
Does a lost path mean I'll find my way?

In the forest of thought, squirrels convene,
Discussing the merits of nuts in cuisine.
If trees took selfies, would they smile wide?
Or lean in close, with branches to hide?

What's the point of a shape without rules?
Are the squares just pranksters, or are they fools?
A compass spins, playing hide-and-seek,
While we ponder the meaning of a little creek.

If I follow the stars, will I reach the sun?
Or just end up in a riddle that's fun?
With each turn around in this puzzling maze,
I might just discover the oddest ways!

Between Want and Wonder

Is it cake or is it fake?
I can't tell with my hungry eyes.
Should I snack or take a break?
This dilemma simply flies.

Do cats really rule the world?
Or just nap like they own it,
With their fur all sweetly curled,
While we toil in our own bit.

Should I binge-watch or go out?
Will I be fit or just a mess?
Endless thoughts, without a doubt,
Until my brain just says "no stress."

In the end, what do we crave?
Answers packed in boxes tight.
But it seems we must be brave,
And embrace the funny plight.

Fleeting Thoughts on a Quiet Day

Why does toast always hit the floor?
It lands jam-side down with a thud.
Should I savor it or moan for more?
Maybe I'll just eat some mud.

Coffee's brewing, but I fumble,
Spilling it all on my good shirt.
Am I awake, or do I tumble?
These little woes always hurt.

Birds are chirping in a line,
Are they gossiping or in search?
They flit and flap, it's just divine,
But I'm stuck in my cushy perch.

Questions dance like shadows flee,
In the stillness of my day.
Yet I laugh, because you see,
That's just how I find my way.

The Longing for Certainty

Do I need a salad or fries?
They both look good in their bowls.
I could just ask the wise guys,
But are they really in control?

When does a cat become a dog?
Or is that just a silly tease?
A barking cat or purring frog?
My brain has bent like branches, wheeze!

Craving answers, I dig in deep,
But often it's just cluttered thoughts.
In my quest, I trip and leap,
Is this wisdom, or lost plots?

Wondering if I should jump now,
Or wait for fate to drop me low?
With a grin and furrowed brow,
I'll just dance in this funny show.

The Tangled Web of Existence

Spinning truths like cotton candy,
Are we sweet or just so sticky?
Life's circus shows can feel quite dandy,
But why does my head feel so picky?

Seeking pathways in a maze,
Dazed by choices, can't decide.
Should I tango or just gaze?
Where the heck's my compass guide?

Juggling dreams with everyday tasks,
How do I balance my own weight?
Even the universe laughs and basks,
At our attempts to contemplate.

Each question spins a new delight,
In the web we weave so tight.
But through the laughter of the night,
We dance beneath the quirky light.

Footprints in the Sand of Time

I walk through beaches, grains in shoes,
Each step I take, another clue.
Waves wash away my little trails,
Do they even care, or just love the gales?

Seagulls laugh, they seem so wise,
As I ponder under bright blue skies.
Is it lunch or are they just pretend?
The questions pile up, will they ever end?

My footprints fade, but where do they go?
Maybe to a party, a sandy show?
I sit and wonder, scratching my head,
While they sip coconut juice instead!

So here I am, a curious chap,
Searching for answers, in a beachy nap.
With every question, the tide pulls me in,
Maybe my footprints are just where I've been!

The Unanswered Echoes

In a canyon deep, I shout my fears,
But the echoes just giggle and disappear.
Hello? Is anyone home inside?
They mock my thoughts, they don't even hide!

Whispers in wind, a squirrel named Bob,
Answers he claims are just a big blob.
I ask him again, a nut in my hand,
He shrugs and tosses it, isn't life grand?

A rabbit hops by, with questions of her own,
"Why is my carrot so far from my home?"
Together we ponder, as clouds drift away,
Are answers just snacks that don't want to stay?

So I laugh with my friends, the critters and breeze,
In this quest for wisdom, we just take it easy.
Life may be puzzling, a riddle of cheer,
But at least in our laughter, the meaning is clear!

A Symphony of Unanswered Whys

An orchestra plays without any cues,
The conductor just lost, confused like the blues.
Flutes trill their why, while drummers just sigh,
Can anyone tell me, oh tell me why?

The violins quiver, their strings in a twist,
"What's the point of all this?" they can't quite resist.
The brass section chuckles, "We just blow hot air,
You answer your question, we just don't care!"

On the stage of confusion, the music takes flight,
As questions keep bouncing, from morning to night.
"Is it A minor, or perhaps C sharp?"
The notes blend together, a nonsensical harp!

So we dance to the rhythm of life's merry tune,
With unanswered whys beneath the bright moon.
If no one knows what's up with this song,
Let's join in the chaos, where we all belong!

Mapping the Uncharted

I unfold a map with scribbles and lines,
Seeking the places where the sun always shines.
But the X says 'oops!' and the arrows all spin,
As I clutch my compass, where do I begin?

Mountains made of candy, rivers of goo,
"Why can't I find my destination, boo-hoo?"
A parrot squawks gossip, in a hat far too wide,
"To find your lost self, just enjoy the ride!"

Crazy trails twist under whimsical trees,
The signs say "beware" but I'm drawn to the bees.
With every wrong turn, I learn with a laugh,
Guess it's not the journey, but the silly path!

So I forge on ahead, with my map upside down,
Navigating nonsense through this quirky town.
With laughter as my guide, and questions a lot,
Who needs a destination, when fun is the plot?

The Enigma of Tomorrow.

Why does the toaster burn my toast,
Yet never dims my sweets the most?
I look ahead, a path unclear,
I trip on dreams that disappear.

The time we waste on silly things,
Like counting fish or buying wings,
With hopes that dance like jumping beans,
And laughter hides in twisted scenes.

I ponder why my cat's so sly,
She rules the house, and I comply,
With every meow a royal decree,
Am I her servant? You tell me.

The future's wrapped in bubblegum,
So sticky sweet, it makes me numb,
I chew and chew, but what's the plan?
Just wing it, that's my master plan.

Whispers of Uncertainty.

Do ducks believe in clouds of grey?
And do they ponder what ducks say?
Questions swirl like autumn leaves,
While squirrels plot and never grieve.

The coffee pot brews thoughts unclear,
As I sip doubts, held close and near,
Why do socks vanish in this space?
They must travel far, or run a race.

The stars above, they wink and nod,
Their twinkling seems a little odd,
Do they gossip about our plight?
Or just enjoy the cosmic night?

In dreams, I chase a wayward cat,
Who leads me astray with every spat,
I giggle at the paths we take,
In search of sense, through every mistake.

The Maze of Our Wonderings.

With puzzling paths and twists and turns,
We search for answers that one learns,
Is water wet? Do trees dream bright?
I'll ask the moon, maybe tonight.

The fridge hums soft, a whisper bold,
It tells of snacks that won't grow old,
I ponder if that cheese could sing,
Or dance a little, just for bling.

I wonder what the fish are thinking,
As they swim by, without blinking,
Do they kerfuffle or plan a coup?
Ah! What's their secret, who knew?

In mazes built of jumbled thought,
We chase the riddles we have sought,
With laughter echoing in our minds,
We're more like jesters than we find.

Echoes of Unasked Queries.

Why do we run when ducks all trot?
And who decided on a pot?
With riddles nestled in each fold,
The stories of the brave and bold.

The sky rains questions from above,
Like free-falling doves, gifted love,
Do ants debate the size of crumbs?
Or are they just waiting for drums?

I ponder the dance of every bee,
They buzz with purpose, wild and free,
Can they solve the math of flowers?
Or just enjoy the sunny hours?

As laughter bounces like a ball,
We question everything, big and small,
Though answers hide like shy old friends,
We'll chase the fun 'til daylight ends.

Beneath the Weight of Wonder

Why is cheese so great yet hard to rhyme?
I ponder this with coffee, every time.
Do socks really disappear in the dryer?
Or do they just seek escape, like a liar?

What's the secret to a perfect pancake?
I flip and flop, oh what a mistake.
Do fish communicate when we're not around?
Or do they just laugh as they swim in their sound?

Why do we worry about what's ahead?
When the cat has mastered the art of bed.
Do shoelaces break out in a dance?
Or is it just me imagining by chance?

Is it true that grass is greener next door?
Or are they just faking a lawn they adore?
So much we ponder, such little will found.
Let's just laugh it off and spin round and round!

Fleeting Moments

Why does time fly when you're having fun?
Yet creeps like a snail when you're on the run.
Is it coffee or truth that keeps us awake?
Or just the existential thoughts we can't shake?

Why do we park in driveways, yet drive on roads?
Asking these questions, I lighten my load.
Do birds ever feel a bit out of place?
Or just celebrate their continuous race?

Do ice cream flavors hold secrets untold?
Or is it just sugar that makes us feel bold?
When do kids think that they grow up so fast?
While parents just wish that those days wouldn't pass?

Why does every answer lead to more queries?
Is it just life's game, filled with funny theories?
We laugh and we question, a shared family jest,
In this whirl of confusion, we find our own rest.

Eternal Searches

What's the deal with socks and their missing peers?
Are they evolving, escaping our fears?
Why is Monday the gloom of the week's well-lit sky?
While Friday tiptoes in, with a wink and a sigh?

Do we really know what makes people laugh?
Or is joy just a math problem, echoing half?
Are we seekers of truths in a world full of fluff?
Or is it just humor that's strong enough?

Why do we sit in lines just to buy food?
Is it a test in patience? A cosmic mood?
Do light bulbs flicker when they dream at night?
Or do they just hum to their favorite plight?

As we chase these riddles, who's really to say?
We've got curiosities sprouting each day.
So let's share a chuckle, make questioning fun,
For laughter's the journey, even when on the run!

Labyrinthine Journeys

Why do we squeeze a whole tube of toothpaste?
It always runs out in a maddening haste.
What's the secret behind cake's delicious appeal?
Is it frosting or mystery that makes it so real?

Do we need a map for the road called 'Perplexed'?
In this galaxy where the guides are perplexed?
Why does my dog act like he's got all the smarts?
While I barely figure out my own missing parts?

When does 'just one more' sound like a good plan?
Especially when pie's within arm's span?
Why does gravity seem to claim all my socks?
While they run off to join those in shoebox rocks?

Will elevators break down if I'm too polite?
Or are they just waiting for a comical flight?
As we wander this maze, let laughter be key,
For in the absurdity, we find all our glee!

Notes from the Edge of Inquiry

Why do we nod as if we understand?
While Google has answers all planned and manned?
Is it just us, absurdly wise in our ways?
Or are we conspiracy theorists for days?

What's with the weather? It never stays still.
One moment it's sunny, then a thunderous chill.
Do ducks have a secret about swimming in groups?
Or do they gossip of toast without any loops?

Why do we sing in the shower with pride?
As if the soap knows each lyrical stride?
Is that reflection really showing the truth?
Or merely the doubts of an uncertain youth?

Let's turn each question into a new comedy scene,
With laughter the punchline, a joy-filled routine.
As we scribble these notes, let's relish the fun,
For in the midst of confusion, we're all still one!

The Enigma of Existence

Why do socks vanish in the wash?
Is it a plot from the laundry's quash?
Why's the pizza always round and wide,
When the box speaks of a square inside?

Is it true that cats plot our demise?
Or do they simply long for our fries?
Why do we trip over our own two feet,
In a dance where we try to look neat?

What's with the smile on a child's face?
Is it magic or just a wild chase?
Why does chocolate fix all our woes?
With every bite, the magic flows?

In this strange world, we twist and spin,
With endless wonders we dive right in.
Perhaps the laughter's the answer we seek,
In the absurdity, we find our cheek.

When Clarity Eludes Us

Why do we always search for the light?
In the fridge, when it's ready for a bite?
Is green really a color or just a hue?
Or did someone mix blue and yellow stew?

Ever wonder why bedtime's so tough?
Are pillows plotting, saying, 'That's enough!'?
What if pillows could talk, oh what they'd say,
As we dream of things that whisk us away?

Is a cat just a furry little sage?
Teaching us lessons at every age?
And if chairs could giggle or bask in the sun,
Would they applaud all the weight they've won?

When questions linger like a stubborn stain,
We laugh till it hurts, through pleasure and pain.
In the fog of confusion, we sometimes see,
That humor might just hold the key.

Musings Under Starlit Skies

Where do the stars hide in the day?
Taking a break, or just lost their way?
If constellations have secret plans,
Are they laughing at us, with their shining brands?

Why do we talk to ourselves in the mirror?
Is our reflection the one we hold dearer?
And do shadows giggle when we trip and fall,
Or keep it a secret, the funniest of all?

If the moon had feelings, would it ever weep?
Or just smile at the dreams that we keep?
Are waves in the ocean just pillows of foam,
Or whispers of sailors far from home?

As we ponder life's twists beneath the stars,
We find humor twinkling in cosmic memoirs.
Perhaps in the questions that keep us awake,
Lies the laughter, for goodness' sake.

The Depths of Inquiry

Do ducks waddle to keep their cool?
Or is it just part of their feathered school?
Why do we ask questions while cooking up heat?
Is it to entertain our imaginary seat?

What if trees chat while they stand still?
Sharing gossip on the breeze, what a thrill!
And is the sun a giant, glowing ball,
Or just a lamp that won't light up the hall?

Why do crayons come in a box so neat?
But always seem short when your drawing's complete?
Could it be that puzzles mock our minds?
As we twist and turn, trying to find?

So here we are, in our hilarious quest,
With chuckles and giggles, we try our best.
In the depths of our thoughts, we dance and sway,
With laughter as compass, come what may.

Whirlwinds of the Mind

Thoughts are like squirrels, so fast and spry,
They zig and zag and ask me why.
Chasing them down feels like a race,
But they vanish quick, without a trace.

A riddle here, a puzzler there,
Why does my coffee always share?
It spills on my shirt, a sly little drip,
And now my wardrobe is on a trip.

Questions float like bubbles in air,
Popping away, oh, what a dare!
Why does the toaster burn the toast?
Is it breakfast or a crispy roast?

So many thoughts bounce in my head,
Like a circus troop, all tightly spread.
But answers run off, they sneak away,
Leaving me jester in this raucous play.

The Unseen Path

Walking a trail that's hard to see,
Is it my feet or my mind that's free?
With every turn, a question blooms,
Are there any maps in these crowded rooms?

Where does this road lead, who can tell?
Is it heaven or just a pizza bell?
One foot forward, trip on a stone,
Hey, that's not my toe—it's a gnome's throne!

Clouds above dance like silly old fools,
Do they witness the secret of our schools?
Why do they tease with shadows long?
Tickling the ground like a mysterious song.

The path is hidden, with twists like a plot,
But I'll keep striding—give it a shot!
For every misstep, I offer a grin,
Who knows what wisdom lies tucked within?

Chasing Illusions

I thought I saw a chocolate feast,
But it was just a muddy beast.
My eyes betray, they pull a prank,
Sipping lemonade from a dirty tank.

Mirages dance just out of reach,
How many lessons can they teach?
Like carrots for a teasing rabbit's chase,
I'm always on the hunt; oh, what a race!

To find the truth, I wobble and sway,
But illusions laugh, and they slip away.
They wear disguises, they change their clothes,
Even my fridge has secrets it knows!

So I'll keep running, though I might trip,
With a grin so wide, I'll never zip.
For who needs answers when fun's the game?
Chasing shadows, it's never the same!

Fleeting Moments of Clarity

In a blink, I see the world just right,
But then it swirls back into the night.
A spark of wisdom, a flash of thought,
And then it's gone, like ice in hot pot.

I ponder deep with my morning brew,
Is my mug talking back, or is it just blue?
With every sip, I try to define,
Why Mr. Whiskers is acting divine.

A joke pops up from time to time,
Spinning around in this curious rhyme.
Like a rollercoaster, it dips and dives,
But brings a chuckle, that's how it thrives!

So here I stand, in my whimsical haze,
Chasing clarity through life's silly maze.
With laughter my guide and questions my map,
I'll waltz through the confusion, and take a nap!

When Questions Become Companions

In the morning, they sip their tea,
While I struggle to find my car key.
They chuckle and nudge, poke at my head,
As I wonder if I left my sandwich for bread.

They dance around in my foggy mind,
Sipping thoughts that I can't seem to find.
'Why do socks vanish in the wash?'
They giggle and flourish, oh what a posh!

Each week they play a new game of tag,
Chasing answers like an old, worn-out rag.
I ask them questions, they roll their eyes,
And respond with riddles and doubtful sighs.

My companions of queries, and curious fowl,
They laugh on the couch, take life as a prowl.
So here we sit, just me and the crew,
As we ponder the meaning of the color blue.

Thoughts that Wander

Thoughts take a stroll when I hit the bed,
They trip on the dreams that pop in my head.
'What's for dinner?' one asks, feeling bold,
While another checks Instagram, or so I'm told.

They skip through the fields of trivial stuff,
Calculating how long cheese should be tough.
A philosopher, one thought, starts to hum,
As the others debate if the cat should be dumb.

They ponder the universe, all vast and wide,
Then decide that a snack must coincide.
As I slumber and dream, they giggle and muse,
In a world of their own, they rarely refuse.

Thoughts that meander, with laughter and cheer,
Ask silly questions and pull me near.
When morning arrives, they quickly take flight,
Leaving me here to search for the light.

The Void of Understanding

In the chasm of thought, where answers escape,
Questions abound, like a slippery grape.
What's up with socks? Where do they flee?
I ask and I ask, but no one's in spree.

The universe giggles, stars twinkle at night,
While I'm here puzzling over petty plight.
My gears are a-turning, yet silence prevails,
As questions mount up in astronomical scales.

Have birds ever debated how to take flight?
Or do they just wing it, from morning till night?
I scratch at my head, and the void just laughs,
As I ponder the nature of silly life drafts.

The empty abyss offers no grand delight,
Just echoes of queries lost out of sight.
Yet I chuckle at the void, my curious mate,
For it's better to question than sit and await.

Unspoken Realities

In unvoiced thoughts, there's a party of me,
Where questions do leap and dance with glee.
Why is there traffic? What's for dessert?
I ponder and joke, with a playful flirt.

Reality winks, as if saying, 'Hey!'
'You wonder a lot, but can't find your way.'
I nod with a grin, give understanding a twist,
The answers all seem to be lost in the mist.

Do clouds ever think of what's up with rain?
Or do they just float, feeling nothing but plain?
They giggle at me, these silent speech thieves,
As I question their motives like rude little leaves.

Yet here's the funny part, dear friend, don't you see?
These unspoken moments, they're just for me.
I laugh with my queries, and share a sly grin,
For the joy in the asking is how we begin.

Shadows of the Unknown

What's the point of socks in pairs?
When one just vanishes into thin air?
I search the dryer, I ask the cat,
But all I find is an old, lost hat.

Why do we call it a 'silent' letter?
It never speaks, just makes me fretter.
I write a word, then I pause in dread,
Are my letters playing tag instead?

If clocks could talk, what would they say?
'Hurry up, or you'll miss the play!'
But moments tick, and don't you dare,
To ask them who's in charge of air.

When did adulthood become a chore?
I thought I'd fly, but I just bore.
I'll take a nap instead of 'grown-up',
And sip my juice from a fancy cup.

Fragments of a Curious Heart

Why do we park on driveways so grand?
While the roads are crying for space to stand?
It puzzles me as I sip my tea,
Questions stack up like shoes by the sea.

How come the sun hides when I'm at play?
Yet blazes brightly on a Monday?
It tickles my toes with a job to do,
And makes me ponder who planned this view.

Why do they call it 'fall' for a season?
When leaves just twirl, it's a dance with reason?
I grab my broom but they laugh and flee,
Maybe I should just join the spree.

Is there a guide to our steps on this quest?
Or do we wing it, just doing our best?
I'll sketch a map with crayon and glee,
And take it camping, just you and me.

Unraveled Threads of Thought

What's that sound? Is it a ghost?
Or just my brain, it likes to boast.
With every twist and every turn,
It overthinks like it's got a fern.

How come cats rule the world so sly?
With naps and purrs, while I just sigh?
They lounge like kings on sunny spots,
While I chase dust bunnies with my thoughts.

Why do we say, 'A penny for your thoughts'?
Shouldn't it be more, for all that we've taught?
Ideas are rich, like treasure maps,
Yet I trade mine for cheesy paps.

Why do we talk to ourselves at night?
Is that why our dreams take flight?
In the land of nod, I find my muse,
Even if she tries to spread the blues.

Gaze into the Abyss of Ambiguity

Why do we eat dessert before our meal?
It makes the spinach seem unreal.
With cakes and cookies dancing wide,
While veggies whisper, 'Don't let go of your pride.'

Do fish get thirsty swimming about?
Or just wave, and then they shout?
With bubbles popping in their way,
"Send us snacks, we love to play!"

Who decided that we need a chair?
When the couch is soft, and who would care?
I sink in comfort, but there's a catch,
My phone's on the table. Oh, what a match!

When do we stop asking 'why' and 'how'?
Asking on a whim, here and now,
Maybe it's fun, it keeps us spry,
With questions floating like birds in the sky.

Whirls of Wonder

Why do socks disappear in the wash?
Are they off partying, just being posh?
The cat sits judging with a knowing stare,
Like it's a secret that we must bear.

Should I trust the fridge light, though it's so bright?
Is it really on when I close the door tight?
Why do I run where I must not be late?
Oh, the wonders we ponder while we wait.

If pies can fly, then why can't I?
Can I throw my dreams and watch them fly high?
Why is my toaster a contraption supreme?
Sometimes I wonder, is this real or a dream?

With all these queries, I giggle and muse,
In this circus of thoughts, I'm destined to lose,
Yet here I am, smiling with irony's jest,
For the whirls of wonder are truly the best.

Tides of Uncertainty

Why do ducks all waddle in a row?
Do they have a leader we just don't know?
If fish can swim with such grace and ease,
Why am I tangled in branches like these?

What makes a sandwich taste better with fries?
Is it all about portions or clever lies?
When did I start wearing socks with my shoes?
Oh, the styles and trends, we always confuse.

Do trees have roots that tickle their toes?
Or a deep conversation nobody knows?
When a pencil breaks and makes me feel blue,
Is it crying out for a sharper debut?

In waves of absurdity, I float and I bob,
With questions so silly, it feels like a job,
But nearly each query brings chuckles and cheer,
Oh, the tides of uncertainty, how they endear!

Comets of Complicated Thoughts

Why does my phone cheer when I'm all alone?
Is it plotting new ways to make me its drone?
If cupcakes could talk, what stories would they tell?
Or are they just baked goods under a spell?

Why do I find socks that are lost in the dark?
Did they join a circus or run off to the park?
When did my coffee become such a creep?
I swear it watches me while I sleep!

Why do we giggle at shadows that creep?
Is it the mysteries we dare not keep?
When time flies by like a comet in flight,
Is it laughing at us in the dead of night?

In this galaxy riddled with curious lore,
I ponder the puzzles and keep wanting more,
Amidst all these comets of thoughts so profound,
I float in the chaos, where humor is found.

The Riddle of Existence

Is it true that cats have nine lives to waste?
Or are they here just to move with such grace?
Why do we giggle at puns that we hear?
Is laughter a way for the heart to be clear?

How can a donut make mornings feel bright?
Is it the sprinkles or just pure delight?
If my plant starts dancing, should I sing a tune?
Or would it prefer to bask in the moon?

What's the meaning behind a leaky old pen?
Is it plotting to drown any thoughts it can send?
When mirrors reflect a perplexing view,
Do they know the answers we never pursue?

In this riddle, we chatter and jest,
With curious minds, we're always obsessed,
And though answers evade in a whirl of fun,
The mystery's charm makes the searching so run.

Threads of Uncertainty

Why is the sky so high and blue?
Did someone just forget to paint it too?
What happened to the socks I once had?
Are they off on a trip, or just a bit mad?

Do trees ever wonder why they stand tall?
Can they hear the whispers of the leaves' call?
Why do we park in driveways, I jest,
And when do we start to really feel stressed?

Why does my cat seem to rule the house?
Should I bow to her or just be a mouse?
Life feels like a riddle without a key,
Or is it just a cat conspiracy?

So here I sit, with questions galore,
Trying to find out what I'm really here for.
But laughter is best, that much is true,
For absurdities make the world less blue.

Paths Yet to Tread

Why do roads twist like a dance on a spree?
And why does my GPS think it knows me?
Should I trust the signs or just follow my gut,
When all I get is a map with a rut?

Do ducks on a pond feel a bit out of place?
Are they pondering dreams in a feathered embrace?
Can a tree truly hold on to its leaves,
Or does it just want to get in on the thieves?

Why do we chase after things yet unseen?
Like socks in a dryer, all lost in between.
Will we ever arrive, or just drift around?
And is confusion where laughter is found?

With paths all around, which way do we go?
Perhaps it doesn't matter, just let it all flow.
For in every misstep, a story unfolds,
With questions like treasures, each one worth its gold.

The Struggle to Understand

Why does my head spin with thoughts in the night?
Are aliens probing, or is this just fright?
Why can't the toaster just know what I'm craving,
Instead of burning my bread, always misbehaving?

Is it normal to argue with socks left behind?
And what's with the dishes, they're surely unkind?
Can a sandwich really taste better when grilled,
Or is this just a trick that the universe willed?

Why do people say "watch the world go by"?
Can we get a refund if all we do is sigh?
Do questions get answers, or just more queries?
Like why does my dog chase down invisible fairies?

Yet in this chaos, we smile and we jest,
Finding humor in why life's such a test.
So let's kick up our feet and just play along,
For in this wild riddle, we all must belong.

Introspection in a Chaotic World

What's the point of musing with coffee in hand?
Is it to solve puzzles, or just make a stand?
Why do we ponder like owls in the trees?
Perhaps we're just meant to float on the breeze.

Is it okay to laugh at the chaos we see?
Like birds with bad landing, who fall from a tree?
Does gravity giggle when we hit the ground?
Or is there a punchline in every sound?

Why does my phone have a mind of its own?
Is it planning a heist or just wanting to groan?
Can spreadsheets tell stories with numbers so neat,
Or is it just an Excel sheet's version of sweet?

So here's to the questions, the silly and bright,
To the answers that flicker like stars in the night.
Let's embrace the madness, and dance in our thoughts,
For chaos is funny, and laughter's not fraught.

The Heartbeat of Inquiry

Why is a cat always in my lap?
Do they plots or is it just a nap?
Why does coffee turn my brain to mush?
Yet without it, mornings feel like a push?

Do socks really have a secret stash?
Where do they go when they make a dash?
Is laundry just clothes trying to escape?
Or fashion's way of playing a prank on tape?

Why do we count on fingers and toes?
When calculators are right there, who knows?
Is the universe one big cosmic joke?
Or is that just how all the confusion spoke?

Perhaps the questions are all part of the game,
Like trying to chase a fart with a name.
In the end, do answers really exist?
Or are they just mysteries wrapped in a twist?

Lost in the Labyrinth of Questions

Why do we stare at the ceiling at night?
Are the stars judging, or just polite?
Is my fridge's hum really a song?
Or is it just saying, 'You waited too long?'

Is spaghetti the best way to twirl?
Or is that just what the chef wants to hurl?
Do socks really come in pairs, or just one?
A rebel has to have a bit of fun!

Do plants scream when I forget to water?
Or are they plotting like a literary slaughter?
Are there secrets held by every pot?
Or just the thoughts of a caffeinated lot?

Why does the dog know when I'm sad?
Is it magic or just being rad?
As we wander through this vast, wild mire,
We laugh at questions, 'cause they never tire!

The Unfolding Paradox

What do ducks really quack about?
Philosophy, or just a scout?
Is the sky blue, or did I misread?
Is yesterday's lunch all that I need?

Why do we count down to celebrate?
When every moment is perfect for fate?
Like a balloon that begs for a poke,
Are answers just jokes wrapped in smoke?

Is my cat plotting an evil scheme?
Or just sprawled dreaming in a sunbeam?
Do ants really take the lead in their troop?
Or are they lost in their tiny loop?

Perhaps the truth is all just a prank,
Hidden behind a Tasmanian crank.
Inquirers wander, looking for sense,
But all they find are giggles immense!

When Certainty Fades

Is toast better buttered than plain?
Do we ever truly see sunshine rain?
Can we ever know the answers, dear friend?
Or is guessing just what we recommend?

Why do we laugh when we stub our toes?
Is it joy, or just how tension blows?
Can the moon feel sorrow for the sun?
Or are they just playing hide and fun?

Do the socks in my drawer conspire?
To leave me always needing a supplier?
Is there a manual for this wild ride?
Or just questions that tickle our pride?

As certainty tries to pack up and flee,
We poke at confusion, full of glee.
In this world of wonders and quirky delight,
We embrace the unknown, and we just might!

Navigating the Sea of the Unfathomable

What's that floating on the wave?
A sock, a rubber duck, or rave?
Questions swirl like tiny fish,
But answers seem to vanish, swish!

Do fish ever wonder about trips?
Or count their scales and make quips?
I asked a clam, but it just blinked,
As if to say, "We're all just linked!"

On the horizon, a dolphin jumps,
With wisdom buried in its slumps,
But all it says is "Catch your breath,"
Then dives away, leaving a mess.

So sail along, though winds may tease,
With every wave, aim to seize,
The zest of questions lost at sea,
Finding laughs in what can't be!

Flickers of Insight in the Dark

In shadows dance the thoughts we ponder,
Like socks that vanish, we just wander.
When I find light, it flickers fast,
Leaving me chuckling at what's passed.

"Why did the chicken cross the road?"
To find a joke or lighten the load?
Each riddle sipped, another gone,
Maybe it's all just a con?

A light bulb blinks above my head,
Did I pay it rent, or just misread?
With each new glow, I feel so clever,
But soon it dims—ah, it won't last forever!

Whispered secrets from the twilight,
Questions bloom with every sprite,
In the dark, we all might peep,
At hilarious thoughts that make us leap!

The Unwritten Chapters of Tomorrow

Tomorrow's tales tucked in a drawer,
I search for answers, but find folklore.
"Did I really eat that last slice?"
Such queries spin, like an old device.

Plans sketched out on napkins, you see,
Glimpse of futures too wild to be.
"Will I fly or trip on my shoe?"
I guess we'll laugh at whatever's true!

In the book of endless mishaps,
A doodle's worth more than mishaps.
The characters giggle, the plot twists tease,
As I write on this page with cheese.

Ink stains mark the hands of fate,
Outcomes uncertain, isn't it great?
With every scribble, I find my flow,
And question whether squirrels also glow.

Messages from the Void

In the cosmos, what do we find?
A voice from nowhere, oh so blind!
"Can you hear me?" it seems to say,
While I'm just munching on my ray!

Thoughts like comets zoom past fast,
Is that advice, or just a blast?
I reply with a wink and grin,
"Is this a game or just a spin?"

Galaxies filled with jokes untold,
Some cosmic humor, brave and bold.
"Life's a riddle," quips a star,
But I can't find my snack from afar.

So I send a note with a wish,
To the universe, in joyous swish.
With echoes ringing in my head,
Laughter floats where questions tread!

www.ingramcontent.com/pod-product-compliance
Lightning Source LLC
Chambersburg PA
CBHW071849160426
43209CB00003B/474